The I in My Eye

Poems by
L.Q. Murphy

Edited by
Kerri Marikakis

Illustrated by
Stacy Hummel

The I in My Eye
Copyright© 2021 L.Q. Murphy

Illustrations by Stacy Hummel

ISBN: 978-0-578-97976-2

- Mom (1961 - 2018)

OF LIFE

Oh jagged sword that lays upon my vein,
Will I face torment another day?

Oh jagged sword that lays upon my vein,
Will thy hurt more than past days' pain?

Oh jagged sword that lays upon my vein,
Will glory come to end my day?

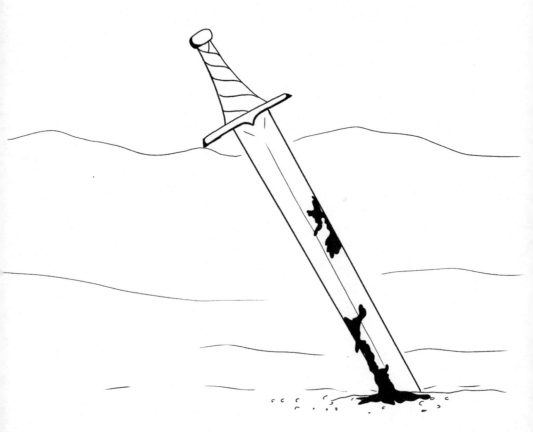

THE GOVERNMENT OF I

I'd rather be killed by the
Glory of the sword

Than by the bloodless ink
Of the king's pen

THE SEEKER

Truth lies between heartache and pain,
And he who seeks truth is surely insane.
For he will be bound to find heartache,
And will thereby suffer much pain for his sake.
Because truth exists in the rivers like gold,
Lying on river beds, filtered and sold.
The truth you seek is more precious than gold,
All haste ineffective, nullified, cold.
The product of exhaustion and stories told,
Beyond horizons stand tall and stand bold.

CLARITY

Where did I leave my sense of life?
To words I ask for clarity.
How do I find my sense of life?
These words I ask for clarity.

Did someone steal my sense of life?
Language falls from clarity.
Should I hide my sense of life?
Language dodges clarity.

Is living high the strongest sense?
Dress me firm in clarity.
Does life require additional sense?
My life is in need of clarity.

Is wise the life of many senses?
To words I ask for clarity.
Is life made up of only senses?
These words I use with clarity.

THE PURSUIT OF REVENGE

Do I chase the venom
That walks up my leg
Beneath the denim?
Or
Cut off my leg
And beg?

OUR OWN BAY

Beneath the sound of cheer,
There hides in us a tear.
Beyond the smile we wear,
There lurks a grizzly bear.

Instincts kick in gear,
Some are in fact of fear.
We wink from time to time,
To save this time from crime.

The boat clashes with waves,
That dock the boats at bays.
Watch the watches tick in waves,
Clones we are from bay to bay.

Around this globe it goes,
To stop, nobody knows.
We do this every day,
At the shore of our own bay.

LIFE DID IT

We transform death to life;
And yet life can kill.
If not by another life;
Your life struck you dead.

WHAT IS TRUTH

Is forever truly real?
Does endlessness exist?
Is my star infinite?
In a universe of timelessness,
Answers are but fool's gold.
From ever-demanding questions,
Can one define existence?
We are forever here I think,
We are forever lost I know,
We will forever search I see,
And we will never truly know.

PIECES

Systems run well with pieces,
Solid is the whole.
Whole is what we are,
Systems run and pieces dull.
Grind! Grind! There's friction,
Oil with cash our soul.
In time oil does nothing,
Our bodies pay their toll.
Throw! Throw! The pieces,
Throw them down that hole.
Bury them in debts,
They never truly had control.

DEEPEST BLUE BY BLOOD

Twist me dry of blood;
Empty out my soul;
Watch my blood run blue.

Where does our blood bud?
I can't see the difference;
Twist me dry of blood.

River's mud pumps winter dreams;
Flowing through creeks and icy streams;
Watch my blood run blue.

Life is held within my sea;
Things we know, not things we see;
Twist me dry of blood.

My secrets lay in waters deep;
Blood falls deep each time I weep;
Watch my blood turn blue.

The sea will take blood by flood;
The flesh on bone within the mud;
So please, twist me of my blood
And watch my blood turn blue.

16

COMPATIBILITY

Tribes worship originality;
Societies worship formality;
Men seek the kingdoms' duality;
But there will always be reality
That leads us unswerving to brutality.

PRISONED SOUL

For I was told
By a prisoned soul
There must be nothing
A soul can withhold.
You should know this fact
That nothing is whole
And rules we must know
We don't forget.
To have something there,
There is nothing here.
So, listen close and be by near,
Something or nothing is my fear.
A prisoned soul we can't forget.
No, this thing is a hole
For I was told.

THE LAND THERE

Hey!
Let's walk the hills of irony
And sail the sea of emotions.
Arriving at the shore of change
And atop the sands of oceans.
The boat we dock on summer's shore
First toe down and forever more.

THE WAR OF OFFICE MEN

The oval of life had met a square.
It shouted and pouted like a grizzly bear.
An ocean sat still that day of war.
Office bay air stuffed with deathly snore.

The inch that was given floated away,
Taken by a worker that faithful day.
One mile later in the razor wind,
One bend, one push, no need to rescind.

One spring eve an idea came about,
And in his old car he drove way far out.
The weight of mind and the thick of time,
The things he missed as he made that climb.

Vomit in circles and head full of fog,
The times he had way back on that log.
The storm thunders in the vows of a priest,
Who knew that his grip could be so weak?

Circus and games, no understanding of life.
How could someone think straight whilst
holding a knife?

He walked into a room - clicked, rotated,
locked.

The office chuckled as he walked and rocked.

I FEEL DEEP INSIDE

I
Up to my current place in time
Feel
Like the ever-falling rock
Deep
Beneath my ocean of emotion
Inside
The riptides of my fears
Crushed
By the whale of decisions made
By
The shore of ridicule and of the twisted
Desire
To be loved and to be desired

RENDER A TOLL

Forcing worth with meaning into these stones,
Ravishing skins to beat into fashion it goes.
Forever chained to the past that always
grows?

Eclipsed by the moments I wish to dispose.

Mercy! Oh mercy! Where have you gone?
Elephants march towards the intolerable dawn.

My roots grow in hell's crevices below.
Neptune's cold pushing closer to the
blue-black crow.

Slithering nearer is that dark-hooded fool,
Inclined to work with that ungodly tool.
Dungeons with chains you hid deep in my
skull.

Expose yourself! It's now time you render
your toll.

UP AND DOWN

Up and down things go

The mountains
The valleys
The hills
The land
Up and down things go

My love
My fears
My hate
My tears
Up and down things go

The joy
The pain
The sun
The rain
Up and down things go

A life
A death
A hold
A breath
Up and down things go
Up and down things go…

FIND THE INNER DRAGON

Face yourself, you'll find a dragon.
Tougher than the oldest wagon.
Taller than the largest mountain.
Brighter than a sunlit fountain.
One soft spot and you do know it.
You know the fate and yes, you show it.
Do it.
Take it.
Your sword jagged to the scales.
Make it, break it. Added to your tales.
Brilliant are the rays.
The rays. The rays. The rays.
They dip into our richest chamber.
Love, iron, and labor. It's our chamber.
Locked in the eyes.
Warm blood thickens on the wrist.
Throw the carcass over flame.
And feed it to our bliss.
Take the ash to the volcano peak.
And sit high near the gods.
Feast with them as the evil speak.
Toss, throw, and blow to the gods.
This ash is thrown in hell.
For eternity.
Time will only tell.

MYSELF

Help me find myself.
I may have dropped myself
Off in the center of the meadow.
Or maybe I washed myself away
In the chilled saltwater bay?
Now dancing past midday
Or maybe I dreamt myself away?
In the deep sleep that endures
The world reflects who and what I say.

KINDLY ONCE AGAIN

Kill me with kindness
Kill me with sin
Kill me in blindness
Kill me once again

More powerful than I
Far richer than thee
Pride be your shelter
My home be the sea

Kill me with kindness
Kill me with sin

Where eyes have seen
The soul was hacked
The tears have gone
The eyes are cracked

Kill me in blindness
Kill me once again

Feathers sear on Mercury's crust
My river of blood is dried to dust
Journeys were many on planet Earth
I'll travel to Venus for what it's worth

Kill me with kindness
I'll kill you with sin

Decide whether a friend or foe
Life goes fast, I hope you know
Come with me, I'll keep you warm
Hurry - quick! Here comes the storm

Kill me in blindness
I'll never kill again

THIS LADY - SHE WALKS

Toss me bricks as I tread water,
And we can both tempt gravity.
This lady - she walks
With what I call a forever golden stride.
When her heels tap the stone tiles,
They give gratitude to gravity's grace.
Will I find the cracks in her sapphire eyes?

For now, I will blind the third eye
Nestled in the craters of my heart.
For when I saw her hawks fly out
From underneath her velvet tarp,
It was like that, but with a slice of crow.

I could not tell
If her intentions were sincere,
So I fumbled getting closer.

Beauty - it's the airborne drug
With no placebo for addiction.
It's weight - as light as my teeth are white
But stronger than Zeus's rage
And can extinguish a flaming soul.

But if to tamper with love's open sails,
Insurance but a message dropped in a wishing well.
That I am addicted to this drug forever more,
And the waves of beauty that crash at my chest
Are too strong for me to put them to rest.

ONE HAND LEFT

I have a question but promise me this,
Can you promise not to tell anyone this?
Who am I that speaks beneath the wooden
crate?

Can you point me out? Go ahead, I'll wait.

I thought for a moment I was my hand,
A hatchet to my wrist, I give to this land.
And again, I looked. My legs - yes, there.
So, I laid before a train. Shut eyes.
Whizzing hair.

Now I have but one hand left. What do I do?
Blast those who told me I could not live
without you.

WALK WE MUST

Drop - Drop,
Slow in your message,
Slow in your tale,
Air could never fill your lungs enough.
Walk.
Because walk we must.
It's over.
Smile and be what you are.

36

HAPPENINGS

And with the sun, the rivers race.
And with the moon, the oceans wave.
And with the water, the leaves grow.
In life, all things do turn and change.
In death, all things remain the same.

37

WATER TO SIP

What came of those wandering vast dry lands?
Blue glistening water refreshing cracked dry
hands.
The earth, he saw a tall pink flamingo fly
On the shore, detaching a scroll from leg bands.
Read, "I followed your footsteps. Take my word
Without regret. I have thought of your flesh,
Now its midnight." Eyes like that of a fresh
Cut lawn, he could see the snakes, now the bird.
Grass was gone. With his palm, he brought water
To his lips. With new eyes, he could clearly
See what seemed like a lake turned out to be
Not more than one last sip of dignity.
Her skin so bright, it made night seem hotter,
Sweating all night thinking what life could

IN THE PATH

Agony wrapped in tissue,
Tossed down the toilet,
Mixed with the waste.
Is all this a wasteful action?
Love bundled in red ribbons,
The gift submits to the clock.
Piling under the weight of love,
Will my material give me love?
And then there is beauty,
The house of cards stacked tall.
In the path of the coming storm,
Which would I rather be?
And where is my violin?
The one that communicates
The feelings for which are
Forever twisting in the storm.
Sound transformed to words,
Meaning lost on the voyage.
I wonder what people mean?
I wonder what to say?

RAINBOWS

```
Rainbows sit on the moon
Rainbows rest in my spoon
Rainbows I have denied
Rainbows splash the great blue sky
Rainbows for the grins so cold
Rainbows for the hate they hold
Rainbows I have within my core
Rainbows I will, yes, ask for more
```

LISTEN THIS TIME WON'T YOU

```
Talk-talk-talk-talk
Talk-talk-talk-talk
Talk-talk-talk-talk
Wait - What?
Listen - I talk - You listen.
Now… What was I saying?
Oh, forget it.
You never listen.
I help and help.
You never listen.
I never had someone like me.
Why don't you listen?
How do you expect to make it?
You never listen.
Repeat what you just heard.
See, you haven't listened.
What if a train were coming?
I would hope you'd listen.
If a beastly herd were coming?
You wouldn't listen.
So, what am I to say
If you do not listen?
I talk and talk.
I advise, you listen.
For what I say,
To those who listen.
It's scoundrels like you who
Never listen.
```

LEAVES GREEN

Leaves youthful green
I learn from you, youth is fragile

Leaves deepest green
I learn from you, seasons make strong

Leaves flattest green
I learn from you, age will make brittle

Leaves fallen green
I learn from you, the grace of death

Leaves not green
I learned from you to cry

Leaves green
I learned from you

THANKING EARTH

Let's walk at the river's edge toe to toe,
Rolling with stones glimmering beneath the flow.
Hear it now – a fly buzz; busy bugs on river crops.
Listen now – tweeting birds; high up in the treetops.
Kicking dirt alongside the working ants,
Thanking earth for this body inside my pants.

MISS VIXEN THE KITTEN

A thunderstorm trotted the lot of Little Ms. Vixen.
The clouds reached down and stirred a great big mixing.
Three large tornados. Ivory columns sky high.
One straight, two leaning. Three howling right by.
The red brick house held a little kitten. Ms. Vixen.
Beauty and innocence clashed in a momentous mix in.
Which is beauty? Which is innocent? Together were they.
Frightened. Shook. Ms. Vixen peeked through her bay.
A paralyzing flash cracked the grey sky for a peek.
Deep in the soul, heaven and life proceed to meet.
Never again to trot the lot of little Ms. Vixen,
Miss little ol' Vixen, the only "red" kitten.

TEMPORARY CHANGE

My grip is temporary,
So try to hold earth with earth.
The lines I see are temporary,
So change is concrete.
The change of things is temporary,
So to never change is the greatest change.
Change will be our fossil
From which spawns understanding
And yet ignorance begins.

TRANSPARENT INK

Write in transparent ink the truth,
The things I search for when I dream in day
And see that you will not have time to tell.
For I will become space and discern you,
Leaving you left with knowledge I never needed
And imbedded in earth where I was seeded.

FIFTY COINS OF SILVER AND GOLD

Fifty coins of silver and gold
Were lost about the winter's cold.
Winter's snow tiptoes to flowing creeks
To fall to rivers from mountain peaks.
Sun brings life to mountainsides
Warm rays assure spring mothers against the tides.
Trout swim downstream as eagles watch above.
Fisherman Jack stands ashore the river thereof.
His net swoops deep. The sunlight helps him see.
Gold and silver coins. Relief. Could this be?
Oh yes, it's so. Fifty coins of silver and gold.
Just to be lost about the winter's cold.

THE MEADOW

I walked into a meadow.
I could see
Greenish-blue water and some trees.
Leaning down, casting brown vines were these.

Ants had a way,
A way to see
The middle. The water clear.
At the bottom, a bed of stones that cobble.

Cobblestones, amongst the smiling catfish,
They could see
There was a red ruby. Large as a pinecone.
The moonlit night reflecting a delicious cherry tone.

Off in the distance, on this day,
I can hear. I can see
A lady tell a boy about something so dear to she.
To her heart. It was part. It would be.

A valuable lesson from an old tall man with a white
beard.
This she could see.
He whispered to her.
"In the middle should be what you can see.
And if it not, beware, no ruby will help things be."

The man waved his walking cane and winked.
This we all could see.
Within our eye, we see our "I."
Amongst the creek of life, the heart in I stay by.

GIGGLES THE MOUSE

Giggles the White Mouse had two red berries,
One a cranberry and the other a cherry.
In the stars of the blue night, he smelled them good,
And asleep he fell underneath the baker's hood.
Before he could see that his berries were gone,
He had dreamed he baked pies before meeting the dawn.
Before his tiny tail shivered him awake to see,
The baker screamed an unwelcomed decree
That Giggles the White Mouse must exit at once,
No cranberry or cherry to take from his hunts.

GIRLY-GIRL AND A FROG

Girly-Girl and Betty-Button found a frog.
Betty-Button's dog sniffed the frog in the log
As Girly-Girl stepped back to get away,
Complaining of warts and smelly decay.
The frog soon turned away and hopped.
Betty-Button followed suit and hopped
Beside the frog down the hill to the creek
As Girly-Girl and the dog looked on with critique.
The lumpy frog jumped in, croaking a goodbye,
That was followed by Girly-Girl's happy sigh.

BIRDS NEST

A blue jay and willow tree grew in the springtime.
The blue jay flapped, and the tree found its prime.
The bird flew about the valley that summer to return
With a talkative cardinal of red, ready to learn.
Learn why willow trees weep in the months of fall,
Months of longer moons and stars of all.
The tree slowly replied with a weeping tear
That fall was a season that took many things dear.
Like our sun that is jailed behind moody clouds
And poppies in willow forests, wrapped in shrouds.
The icy wind pricks sharper than thorny vines
And we are merely shadows outlined by lines.
The blue jay and cardinal knew none of this
And agreed with the old willow a problem exists.
That night, the birds slept in the branches of the tree
To think and to dream of the seasons to be.
The blue jay and red cardinal awoke in joyous delight
With ideas that had churned and turned overnight.
If they began now, they could build a large nest
That could hold food for winter and be pleasant to rest.
The two got to work and built their nest on the highest branch,
Tall windows to watch the winter pass and the farmer's ranch.
They stored berries and counted black oil sunflower seeds.
The willow tree swayed with joy, knowing love supersedes.
Fickle surroundings that party in the light when things are bright,
Then make way to other lands when the twilight's in sight.
But the most important thing the willow tree learned
Was that a winter without weeping would soon be his turn.

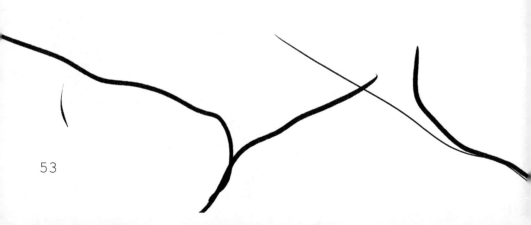

MR. SUNNY SUN

Mr. Sunny Sun eclipsed the mountaintop
Where the green ferns grew around the fountain shop.
He watched his towns come to life beneath his eyes,
The rays exposing animals shooing buzzing flies.
Brown bears, peacocks, and pigeons galore,
Bicycles, skates, marbles, and more.
Alligator scales green and white grew hot,
Dragonflies diving through a misty spot.
Where river water splashes the warming docks
And kids hop around skipping pancake rocks.
But before Mr. Sunny Sun could say goodbye,
He awoke Mrs. Moon, who always stayed nearby.
Mrs. Moon watched furry animals curl up to sleep,
Making room for her nighttime creatures to creep.
An old cricket saluted as his brittle legs screeched
And the bats that awoken had yawned and reached.
Brown rats counted fruits and berries to eat
While nearby foxes sniffed cold dirt at their feet.
Many say night creatures are scary, but it often depends
Because Mrs. Moon would not hesitate to call them her friends.

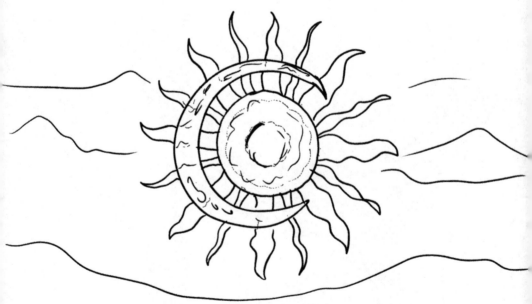

SEA BIRDS CHASE

The sea birds chased the undecided shore.
Sugar to my eyes,
Tears so sweet.
It just happened,
The earth, the first apple tree.

THE WEIGHT OF LOVE

Two lovers galloped through a field.
Open. Green. A field with two hills.
Lover One carried a shield.
Lover Two carried love that killed.
They were given a blank gravestone,
The moral of the story unknown.
Now they are bronze statues
Wrenched into a mold.
Stuck by the weight of love
Inside their souls, I'm told.

SAGES KNEW

It was like birth.
Stones cracked under hooves,
Flutes set in motion,
Life and wind carried its tune.
Destiny had no say
And seasons had no part.
Water splashed with wine,
Grapes poured downstream
To the village of the sages.
Rocking in chairs of oak,
Leaves singed orange,
Pipes made of elder pine,
Gaze set upon the bronze.
Clouds whispered by the body
As the sages pondered.
Birds of brown and gray
Talked to nightingales.
Hounds gave homage.
With a nod, sages concluded,
Not one word at all spoken.
The sages knew of beauty.
It was light on skin,
Delicate as a snowflake.
So away they went to sleep
And promised not to dream.
Between mountains they lay
In a long valley of green.
Under the river granite,
Now forever they lay.
With beauty always, they will stay.

I CARRY

For the red ruby that sits in the riverbed,
I carry, with sore shoulders, blankets of silken thread.
For the river stones that guide life to my valley well,
I carry, on blistered soles, the finest zinfandel.
For the wise falcon that preserves the bluest skies,
I carry, on bending knees, a map from the most wise.
For the howling wolf die-casted in the eye of the moon,
I carry, with beating heart, warm flesh of my beast platoon.
For the virgin snow of white that is transformed into water,
I carry, in a stringed satchel, friends from yesteryear.
For me, the lonely soul who went missing many suns ago,
I carry a fool's vision searching for the perfect plateau.

THE WISHING WELL

What is the purpose
of the wishing well?
The wishing well?
Yes, the wishing well.
Couldn't tell, but I've heard a tale
Of the basin wishing well.
It rotates from Summer's June
To Spring's farewell in May
From the wishes that dwell.
I'll tell you, young guppy,
I have touched the well
During Winter's afternoon,
Feeling the pain
Of the wishers who came.
I asked what purpose
The wishing well serves.
Answer…it serves to ease life's curves.
It's to shatter the sickles
That rip apart our happy nerves.

EACH CHAMBER OF THE HEART

A ballet of butterflies
Danced in each chamber of my heart.
Flying through my skin,
Took the ferry on the blue blood river.
Spies against native blood,
Through the double valve they rocked.
With speakers loud they spoke,
Instruments played,
Eyes still mesmerized.
They anchored in the chambers, now red.
The boat swayed and the foreigners stood,
Round the hull in ballroom dance.
The essence of fools falling in love.

JUMP

Jump over the officer's swinging baton.
Jump high enough to hitch a ride.
Jump off a roof onto the passing bystander.
Jump up and grab a witch's broom.
Jump to jump so that you feel good.
Jump high to brittle branches where millions lurk.
Jump about the world on a pogo stick.
Jump to heaven and put in word of salvation.
Jump in the fire that burns where your parents work.
Jump with the executives that celebrate our fall.
Jump into your bed to dream of fiction.
Jump awake in hopes of a painless day.

LEAVE MAN THE REST

Take the clouds from the sky,
Take the salt from the ocean,
Take the feathers from the birds,
Take the scales from the fish,
Take the milk from the mothers.
And what's left?
Leave man the rest.

IF I HAD A TURTLE SHELL

If I had a turtle shell,
My life would be so very swell.
Right outside the gate to hell,
I am awakened by its bell.

Artichoke skin. Layered tight. No light.
Travel shielded better than a knight.
Spin the world to see things just right.
Chomping on justice. Stationed. Ready to bite.

Carry my home upon my boulder back,
Roaming past home with a killer's rack.
My long-tailed friend named Shuffling Jack
Now sleeps with trash near a burning sack.

Live long to see the flaws root deep,
Outside the sun's rays pound and creep.
The tree that grows from that root will keep.
When it dies there, there will be no weep.

TEASE LADY JUSTICE

Can change linger outside of reach?
Forever and one day more?
Change so hidden that my simple eyes
Cannot catch his silhouette?
The good change I seek,
If there be such a thing,
Floats about the room I occupy.
Waiting-motionless-curious
At the dinner table.
It watches me eat
With scientific eyes,
Not sure what to make of me.
Taking notes,
Never leaving - Never far,
It must know the change I need.
It orbits me,
Captivated by my heart's desperation.
Silent in the air it sits,
No expression, but just there
With what I need
In its hands.
Facing me like a mirror's reflection when I sleep,
Blink-less eyes stare as I count sheep.
Oh change,
I know it thinks to leave,
Roaming the world in a morbid sleepwalk.
It will someday,
Hesitant at first,
But soon towards the horizon.
Onto the courts of the land
To tease Lady Justice at her den.

LIFE GOES TO THE NEXT STOP

Glass clings take flight and land in ears,
Memories pulled out by rolling tears.
Laboring saws cut down regret with beers,
Yearning for rising suns of cheers.
Faster and faster, changing rusted gears,
One up, showing off to our valued peers.
Slender daggers rest, conversing with spears,
Traversing blazing forests, blinded with sears.
Battle eyes look forward, never minding their rears,
To painted visions of amusement turned to smears.
Brakes absent as the great wall appears,
Lost on a ladder of pooled careers.
High maybe, but green clouds blur frontiers,
Life's policy to do good never adheres.
Bubbles, cracks, and bends – our premiers
Chase, fumble, and bypass our mental spheres.
Our reason dropped in transit, so many years,
Gravity and mirrors do meet our denial and fears.
Down our black brick road to medical engineers,
Giving soul and right arm to trusted financiers.
Our delicate butterfly of youth reappears,
In peacetime the tick-tock clock interferes.
Our dim hope sets with the sun and disappears,
A keen diet of pills given by local cashiers.
Soon enough, Deep Rest we go, leaving only souvenirs,
Next stop, heaven, in clean Jeep Waggoneers.

AWAY AND FORGOTTEN

A lean boy sat on a wooden dock.
Fish jumped about still water - flies buzzed.
Wind rolled free over the aquatic mirror.
Clouds unrolled as the sun pushed the earth 'round.
Fire and ice bound about the land and sea.
Like their cousin's spring flower and bumble bee.
Bolted silver daggers gripped by golden gloves.
Capitulated heart under broken ribs of wood.
Down the sacred aisle, scabs fall like rose petals.
Drifting from the dock, hair falls as life fades.
Away. Forgotten. A pebble in beach sand.

ASLEEP FOR GOOD

Beyond my crossing blue veins,
My heart must have jumped a million times.
Stuck behind my brown eyes,
My mind must have tried to escape a billion times.
Beyond my skin is but earth blended together,
The good, the evil, the warm, and the cold.
Beyond the walls of my house,
No clouds, no fog, no rain, or sunshine.
Beyond my grinning teeth
Is a severed tongue sliced clean by morality.
Beyond my handmade shoes
Is nerveless skin that ensures survival.
Underneath my midnight black gloves
Rest lifeless hands flurried by thoughts.
Beyond the walls of my arteries,
Poison pumps warm to brain and limbs.
Beyond the wooden roof beneath the grass,
We fall asleep for good at last.

DISABLED SCENE

Sizzle humid air,
Frantic frizzled hair,
Damaged wooden chair.
Evil burning spear,
Chasing after deer,
Swimming against fear.
Quicksand graveyard there,
Throwing any prayer,
Diving birthday bare.
Arriving at nowhere,
Forewarned to beware,
Nothing I compare.
Shouldn't I declare,
Lacking in childcare,
Decrease the homecare.
Drifting him elsewhere,
Boulders hit glassware,
Falling to despair.
Busting our cookware,
Grabbing the eyewear,
Meager the footwear.
Trample the giftware,
Begging for healthcare,
Mustn't we repair.
Merely figments we compare
In this great disrepair.

I AND TWO CROWS WATCHED

It had been fifty years in the gully,
And the eagles still soared briskly over the leaving
fog.
Our dog Henry had barked his last bark.
My Pa had told my sister Anne to stay upstairs.
I saw her curtains sway in sorrow,
Like death had breezed on by.
The sun was graveyard orange.
So, I and two crows sat on the oak branch.
We watched and when the time came,
We spoke in tune with the moment,
Swept together by the twisting wind.
Prayer sprayed. Volcanic dust.
Lava poured from the corner of my eye.
Dragon-like flies darted to the morning rose.
Steer bells cracked the silent land.
Heartache came. Dragon breath upon my conscience,
Chopping at my back,
Dicing my soul.
My wet-nosed friend lay with the dandelions.
Now they grow a bold yellow,
Radiating like the sun,
Warming my cold feet back to life.
My audacity to smell the sweet misery of death.
For Henry's death, I receive his last passion.
Nourish my memories. Pedal to pedal.
Latching to pollen. Bees buzz and whip.
Forever reinstate memory for Pa.
Natural wind. Anne will sway.
Two crows diverge the sky.
Each day, a brighter flower to savor.

WHO IS DRIVING?

Journeys for me have been many.
Swinging axes. Dicing words.
They are forced at times.
Harm be the good of others.
But like others, I have always been in touch.
On the road I travel. Hot roads. The sting of travel.
Maybe the driver upstairs is lost.
But I, the tire, know of cold.
Of moving fast
And getting nowhere.
I stick to something. That vice grip of control.
Knowing if it were not for me, the driver would lose
control.
I'm going flat. A sloppy grip.
Fills me up with hot air. The driver.
I mean, I go through mud and steer dung,
And for what?
Not a care… no pay… no fare…
No Fair!

71

AGING AGAIN

To be tossed when I become bald,
Wrinkled - cracked - weathered.
I may be old, but I know the road.
Never mind the young one you seek
With the softer touch
And the flourishing smell.
Maidens know
Nothing I know.
Now I lay here with no driver,
Just other old things like me.
Some are punctured deep,
Waiting to melt away,
To be reincarnated into something useful.
I watch from the line I stand in
With an alarming stare.
I am no longer a beautiful round curve.
No longer can I keep up with the young ones.
This road on which I settle is new,
Something not said in years.
I have never seen nor heard of this road
But
Deep where the wires run about
And the memories of fertile days root,
I know with suffocating truth
This road may be my last route.

THE MIND OF WIND

Where has the wind been?
Ask the wind where
The leaves chattered on its approach.
This mid-summer day the wind said,
"I say to myself you are a friend,
But I keep no memory of where I have been."
Far west. I pointed. It had came.
The wind was told. The wind ceased.
Brief in time was a windless moment.
Windless. Brief in time was the moment.
Move; it began. The breeze howled about a blade of grass.
Its high velocity formed a reverberating glee. The wind said,
"But faint friend, I can describe what I have seen."
The wind twisted with an angry force
Until I found myself standing in its chest.
In there, there was clarity and calm
Beyond the bend of its balm.

73

ENJOY INSTEAD OF ASK WHY

A rumbling voice shook my gut.
It said, "Shadows large and small
Migrated from deep blue to clear teal.
Creatures from black to rainforest green
Dashed from hollow log to mushroom canopy.
Gray clouds of the burning hill. Death to life came again.
Other clouds bore tears to land that couldn't see the sea.
Dirt fertilized by death. Life grows rampant.
Vineyards that pop violet grapes for the finest wine.
Rolling hills painted by golden hay.
Cocoa-colored fields plowed into fertile nurseries.
Mountain peaks wearing caps of cotton.
Bighorn sheep that ram with the thrust of thunder.
Green pastures where the humans mingle.
And on benches of wood,
Some gazed on like statues of stone."
The wind laughed a hollow drumming cheer.
Then a peaceful blue caught my eye.
It was an image I had of a time when I was but a boy,
before I could wrestle my stupor away.
The wind had gone, leaving me with puzzle pieces.
To this day, that peaceful blue was but a carrot on a string,
And I am a man who has chased it from youth to rusty joint.
From high mountain peak to valley low,
Now the carrot of orange is nothing more.
It is black, crusted with pulverizing fungus.
I don't want it anymore, yet still it lingers nearby.
So, if you catch a summer's breeze,
I recommend you enjoy instead of ask why
Because day turns to night and passes by.

YOUR HEART WITH MINE

Can I say a violin plays in each chamber of my heart?
And canaries flutter in the belly of my soul when I am near you?
Just the touch of your skin can turn stone to water.
Just the blink of your eye can pull me close.
Waters run deep in my river of nerves.
Roses bloom every time I breathe in beside you.
I've seen angels dance in marble halls when you walk the land.
Symphonies play when you speak to the creatures of this world.
And love be not strong enough to fulfill what I feel for you.
And chains of silver and gold cannot keep me from wanting you.
Neither Army nor Navy stands in the way of holding you near.
Stars shoot across the night skies whenever you smile,
And the wolves howl every time you leave my sight.
And never in a million years shall we ever depart,
From flesh to dust I hope to always be a part of your heart.

75

PONDERING A LIFE HAPPIER THAN MINE

I stopped myself before,
But I could not shadow the brave.
The language of the body,
A scheme in its own design.
Brilliantly washed in the dropping sun,
Pondering a life happier than mine.

REST A SEED

In the eve of warming days
Rests a burrowed seed
From the audacious trees
That anchors to feed.
In forgotten plains of North,
It will claim its deed.
Roots to stem to seed is growth,
Freed by breed, and by breed, then freed.

NOW YOU SEE IT THEN YOU DON'T

He pulled his legs tight,
Quite it was.
He never looked to his right,
Quite he is.
He has left far from sight,
Quite I am.

NOW YOU SEE IT THEN YOU DON'T

Water swamp view,
Flat as diamond sides.
From behind stump and dew,
Rises straight up guys.
Scopes wet but still new,
Barrel straight at me dries.
Shocked by the human crew,
End and respect collide.

TWO MOONS THIS NIGHT

She lay in light of kings and pharaohs.
Green eyes bright in white cream.
Hair that flowed like creeks over stones.
Far was her sight with the rays of gold.
Her ears in tune for the screaming owl
That did take flight two moons this night.
Her king now dead and blown about,
Her honest love now an itch of doubt.
Never may be aware she is free.
That she will give up kingdom and peace
To dock with him, finding peace in her eye,
The charm that she used to set him free.

THE TOGETHER MOMENTS

Run with me into the coming clouds.
Let us shower in the earth's tears,
Ripping away our cotton mesh.
Let the leaves rhyme away our years,
Dancing alone together through ponds.
Let our heat evaporate fears,
Cleansing away the mask that dawns.
Let thunder rumble with our cheers.

OPEN AND VAST

Out, open and vast,
Hated orange and flat.
Steps push and pull,
Posturing rippled sand.
Orbiting landmarks trail,
Day dims through gloss.
Cannot sense time of life,
Cloudy day or sun drop.
Soft pull, but greater push,
Falling deep within sand.
With the shadows and dust,
And the less traveled land.

BAD ATTRACTIONS

Earth and wood. Our home on land.
Heart be wiser in my hand.
Bend the stone for the sand.
The home is wood. The love is bland.

Snakes grow from her hairs,
Frozen, stiff, and all alone.
Covered with my coarsened hairs,
Making lookers like silver stone.

Never should get close to you,
Fear of the scratch and to attach.
Snakes and hairs are all for you,
Dance a twirl to get your match.

Sight be terrible close but clear,
But from afar your love is toast.
Freeze you dear to keep you near,
Our life be kindest near the coast.

WHENEVER WORDS FAIL

I would like to speak
Of worlds and gravity.
And of motion within motion
With sincere tongue and divinity.

But who so ever hears my words,
Seated among pieces of wisdom?
Beneath the weight of ocean waves,
Distilling the tears to come?

Bold I dare to be with speech
Of higher altitudes and canopies.
And of thought within enduring thought
With societies on bended knees.

But whenever words endurance fails,
Stand yourself among the growing trees.
And live life like the great blue whale,
Gliding through your worlds and seven seas.

THE ANCHOR OF LOVE

Find structure harmonious.
Obviate the bends,
And drop my anchor here.

Split the second in twos.
The moment I met you,
So, I see our love be true.

Storms will be sure to come.
With flux of highs and deathly lows,
Yet still I choose to anchor near.

For those are days the shores do shine.
My vessel, my captain, and my crew,
Will anchor here forever with you.

THE TOWN

Blizzard with me across the town,
Let our icy walls melt away.
In April, one spring valley day,
Let's flow together cross the town.

To the rose bed park that is uptown,
Lend our legs to trot that way.
Dispelling red petals day by day,
Passing the geese we find downtown.

Watch the world turn from high-town,
Hand in hand to the seas we bound.
Waving softly at the shores,
Whales. Otters. History and wars.

Mirror stars. Mirror owls. Mirror more,
The lights breeze by the lover's core.
Grace be yours. Forever play,
Old town. New town. Low-town we stay.

TIME AND BUILDING LIFE

```
Here it comes to me,
Or do I come to it?
It is coming faster,
I may not think of it.
Flashes of scenes to be,
Of better times supposed be.
Solid in my solid,
Collide solid with me.
```

WILL YOU DO IT?

What to say
About the pearls above?
Can I dare say
I am an emerald of love?
That lays deep
In a mountain lake.
That is wave-less blue
And cradled to keep.
In a stone-less bowl,
A treasured thought
That might cause you to leap.

CAREFUL UNDERSTANDINGS

Can your kitty cat roll and romp?
I know your prissy kitty cat can tromp.
Use it to get some sparkly things
Or just keep it close and attract some wings.

What's your preference on this day?
For it depends on what sins are at bay.
The puppies will grow and smell you too.
The dog pound they walk is not that new.

Purr with your warm fur and stay soft.
Hiss at the dog that roams past your loft.
Arch your back, make them watch the curve.
Growls will come your way, so observe.

Round eyes get you food and shelter.
Groomed to your standards. Helter-skelter.
Do only what is your idea or leave,
Back out the door with eyes that deceive.

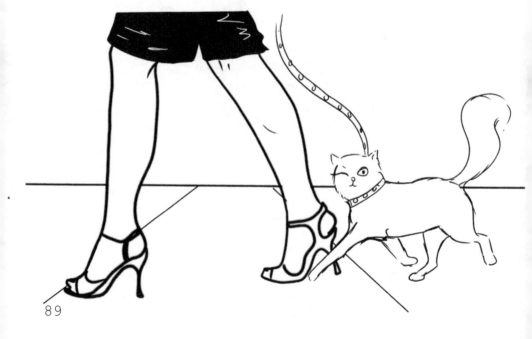

MOVE AND USE

Eat breakfast with the three old bears,
Or have lunch with an old wolf of years.
Or I could just go and roam the earth,
Helping the land expand its birth.

Days ago, I thought of big gold pillars.
Hours ago, thinking of why I need silver
mirrors
That would tell me I could at this moment fly
The god of goddess content made to lie.

Stroll down the minute I am in,
Move my body in dancing sin.
Swaying left to right, right by my rut,
Left to dance merely hut to hut.

Chest held high and chin exposed,
Brick home inside wood fences closed.
Telegrams rushed to me over weeks,
Enemies now roam my high peaks.

WITHIN THE TIME

Within the whole of day, I beg for your touch.
Within the time of sunlight, I search for your affection.
Within the whole of night, I thank the gods for your presence.
Within the time of darkness, you are my ever-burning candle.
Within the waking hour of my day, my heart beats to find you.
Within the hour the sun peaks, I labor to hold you once more.
Within the hour before sleep, I see a picture of you for peace.
Within the minutes of the day, you are always in my mind.
Within the seconds I pray for another second left of time.

I AND SHE

I screamed.
She cried.
I quaked inside.
She looked at me.
I looked away.
She asked questions.
I contemplated.
She arose from her chair.
I shifted in my seat.
She walked into the kitchen.
I listened for her feet.
She cried.
Oh, did she cry.
I stood to my feet.
She pushed a knife through my rib.
I screamed in agony.
She screamed as tears dropped.
I dropped to the ground…

THE TRUTH CAUGHT YOU

She pulled the knife out,
Striking again
And again.
I watched the pain splat.
She uttered signs and signals.
I watched the blood dilute.
She said, "How could you?"
I said, "This is me."

"This is who you are?" she said.
She pulled on her hair.
I reached out my hand.
She turned away.
I struggled to keep a clear image.
She grabbed a gun in her rage.

"I want to see your end," she said.
She looked down at the gun.
Down at the gun… a message to send.

"Please. I cannot tell you the rest," I said.

I was at Death's door.
The floor was cold.
But I was bold.
For I was the boldest
At the door of old.
A brittle day.
A day so cold.

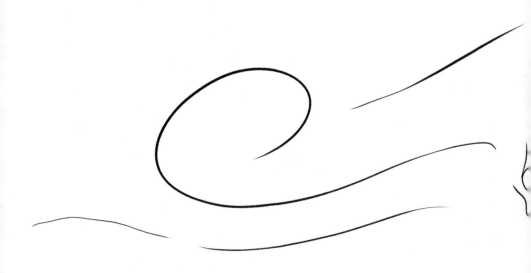

TOGETHER TELLING STORIES

Come with me to have a beer,
But not before we shed a tear.
I know we've had a crazy year,
Let's not be shy and lend an ear.

There are tales and stories we should hear
Of happy things and things we fear.
So grab a smile and abandon your sneer
And gather 'round this fire here.

As I have a story you mustn't miss.
It's one you surely cannot dismiss.
About a queen who lived in inaudible bliss,
Later destroyed by a lover's kiss.

And from my words you will get many things,
Like dancing lions and laughing kings.
You may like deception and some flings,
Or maybe you'll adore the diamonds and rings.

What about the precious musical strings,
Plucked into harmony for ambient springs?
And wait till you hear about vultures' wings
And the cradle littered with cracks and dings.

But for now, let's go ahead and do one thing.
Let's gather real close and make a ring.
And open your ears as I start to sing
Of a maiden who found a fallen king.

96

TREE IN THE SEA

Fourteen leagues beneath the sea
There was no telling what there would be
But I never expected to see a tree

From the dark, creatures began to glow
The underwater wind, yet but a blow
I held on tight, watching the seabed grow

Out crawled a crab with brittle legs
I could see it guarding a mound of eggs
Walking slanted as if its legs were pegs

Then came a fish that snarled and snapped
I wanted to move, but I was handicapped
I tried and I tried, but I did seem trapped

From the dim light, a shadow appeared
I'll be eaten for lunch – that's what I feared
I just wriggled and shook as it slowly neared

Its teeth were gnarled, and one eye was patched
The sea floor stood still except the egg that
hatched
But a whale of a shark swam on by, unmatched

Only then could I see the floor real clear
A passageway – A new frontier
So I gathered my bag and the rest of my gear

I took a photo that gave the floor a flash
Time was running short, so I had to dash
Kicking away with memories of the clash

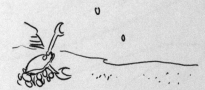

IT - IT - IT

IT began as a dream.
Whatever I choose to call "IT,"
IT knows how to use me,
IT knows how to lose me.

The mind bellows. The eyes do roam.
Crickets relieve the silent fight.
Stars gaze down upon my home,
My home reflecting twilight.

Peace had settled upon my dome,
The memories of IT beating like waves.
Language echoed between my ears,
As IT did slip away.

On the walls there was art drawn bright,
You and I with IT; family and more.
I followed the story along the wall
Until I hit an invisible door.

My eyes could only corner the turn.
IT was good, IT was happy - How will IT end?
So tonight, I lay awake thinking of IT
And the future that IT is meant to extend.

WHAT DO I MEAN?

You know,
There was a time when
I saw roses
Instead of thorns.
There were moments when
I would let go
Instead of feel comfort in the thorns.
There was one chamber
Deep beneath my ribs
That was filled with Hope.
No ice. No stones.
There were nights
Occupied
By the noble dreams of loyalty,
Adventurous journeys.
What happened?
I know Time is nearby.
Change knows me from the past,
But Hope and Dreams are but vagabonds,
Vacant from the pillow I rest,
What do I mean?
At least that is what I tell the rest…

LIFE IMPLIES OTHER

I always feel safer on my bay.
Although beat flimsy, I still stay.
By emotions crashing waves
That protest and never stop.
How did they begin?
How did I?
Giving you a compass
Is but useless in a world made to end.
For what you seek and can be found
Will be crushed to a distant memory,
No more than an echo.
Reverberating in the deepest, darkest caves
Where death can be found meditating,
Deeply dazed by his graceful deeds.

WHERE THE GARDEN STOPS

Ravens gathered 'round the dead King's crown.
Ships moored for the tears of the Sapphire Queen.
Peasants gulped liquid grains of gold in the streets of town.
The land thieved and shadowed by eyes never seen.

Banished to boneless hills beyond the phantom everglade.
Swamps filled with flesh of territorial wingless beings.
Icy eyes cracked by the strike of the bladed raid.
Eyes shut to forever behind the King's blade swings.

And when there be no mirror to show what she demands.
And when there be no peasant to make her feel tall.
Did the Queen think to confirm the image of her land?
Does she see now the garden stopped at her wall?

Earth made the swamp for all kingdoms to know.
How could a queen not navigate her own kingdom?
She begged and screamed to say it wasn't so.
Everyone knew but her this day was destined to come.

POOR DESTINY

Poor, Poor Destiny.
Chained to a cube of steel.
Transported from sea to sea.

You're on a wooden ship.
Fix the holes in your sails.
You must make it back to me.

Poor, Poor Destiny.
Free Will has taken your place.
I beg, I beg you to win this race.

You're on a wooden ship.
Water reached upon your helm.
It must be that Free Will.
Yes, your craft is overwhelmed.

Poor, Poor Destiny.
You're on a wooden ship.
This cannot be your destiny.
Unless this be your last trip.

DEATH POOLS (GET IT?)

Splash! Splash! Splash!
I am drowning.
I am...

Could it be I am not dying?
I must be swimming.
I am not dead.
For there is nothing left to dread.

Swimming be simple.
Look! Look! Look at me float.
I float! I float...look!
Here comes my boat.

Poor Ma. Poor Pa.
I wish you were here.
Don't worry, I'll give homage
For the death you endured...

YOU SINK DOWN

I am light as a feather.
The boat has now arrived.
Ma? Pa? How were you revived?

I saw you sink down,
Down with the crew.

The CREW is aboard!
How did they get here too?

Splash - Splash
We seemed to have drowned.
Splash - Splash
We never made a sound.

If I am,
If I am,
I'll do it now.

If I am,
If I am,
Watch me here.

I can finally swim,
Swim without effort.
I can finally swim,
Swim without fear.

PAIN WANTS SO MUCH FROM ME

Trace me
Chase me
Trip me
I'm yours

Slap me
Lick me
Taste me
Indoors

Failure
Crush me
Heavy
I'm torn

Running
Ducking
Bleeding
Once more

PEARS UNDER THE APPLE TREE

I found pears beneath an apple tree.
The pear will do, although apples be.
And what shall I do about the weeds?
Brought to seeds spread around the trees.
Planted the seeds in no place that burns.
A score of moons later, I returned.
Apple tree, two men taller, twigs about.
Pear tree, two decades smaller, twigs without.
Now the apple I desire,
Short on line. Life's reach is smaller.
For my child the pear, be stern.
An apple tree, to further learn.

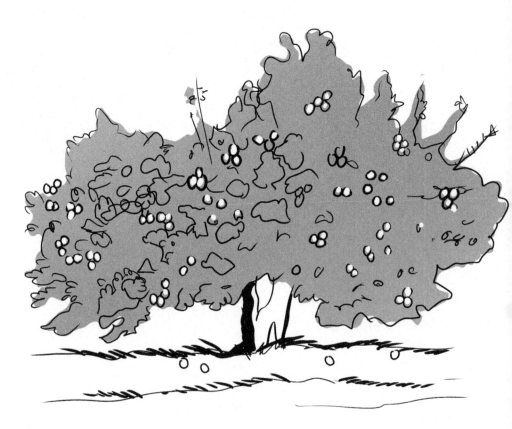

BRUTAL BALANCE

And seas did gallop above the sand,
Taking life we greatly need.
Repeating cycles of torn peace on land,
Splashing always the timeless seed.

If home floats away along with the wave,
Will memoirs fade on this great hill?
Or will the earth beat its very last wave,
Leaving us with a tearful still?

Feet flutter to and fro the tide,
Earth beats for us lost on land.
Your pulse, our most essential guide,
Strides shorter in endless land.

Wind will inflate the thinnest sails,
Blowing away death's only gifts.
Beat forever more amongst the whales,
For time forever drifts.

THE MONEY BALANCE

The little money I have
I spend, spend, and spend.

On widgets, hopes, and dreams
All sins, sins, and sin.

So, let me spend, spend, and spend
So I may forget my sins of sins of sins.

DELICATE GOLD

I have always wanted gold,
A brilliant piece of earth to hold.
To wear for others to behold,
But what is it that must be sold?

To create the greatest story ever told,
Must I wait for years of old?
Until my body's blood is cold?

What is it that I shall withhold
During moments that I must be bold?
Who in the mirror must I scold
To convince the best choice is to remold?

The always endeavoring tales foretold
About the grassy hills and mountains patrolled.
Constantly fighting time's clenching chokehold
Yet all I wanted was some gold.

Must I tell this story sevenfold,
Hugging this story into a mold?
Accentuating its beauty with marigold,
Its radiant rays never oversold.
Within islands and seas, my centerfold.

Now back to vacant roads I've strolled
To find a delicate weight of gold.

NO MATTER

Oh, pity me, oh pity me.
How can I be without the sea?
Light is given as I sow.
Will things I start now ever grow?

Although I might see things appear,
I never doubt a listening ear.
With thorns I cross and horns I face,
Near the very front of the great rat race.

A fickle sea, a sickle cell,
Went too well with my heavy shell.
I've seen it once and maybe twice,
All I know is that it was nice.

If I do fall one sudden day,
Let it be known I reaped no pay.
For life is but a pulsing song,
And when it's done, with earth we belong.

Although I do watch the trees from afar,
The flesh is locked by a see-through bar.
Thick or thin bar I cannot tell,
If the clash of leaves will in fact rebel.

THE SEA STORM OF LIFE

The sea was vast, the sea was bright,
And on this day, he had no light.
No fire, no wood, no leaves, no flare,
Tall that night in cool dripping despair.

A splash, a boom, a crack that day,
A crash, a wave had washed him away.
He swam, he sank, he tossed, and tanked,
On a big whale fin he desperately yanked.

Pulled with might and force, the whale then
spouted,
Riding the waves as dolphins pouted.
Shrunken old man and his little feet,
Making home on so very little to eat.

Chilly teeth made a chitter and chatter,
Ice-crusted nose led nerves to batter.
Tummy did growl for oven-baked crab,
Soon calling the critters he could grab…

TO SEE THE SEA OF LIFE

There was dark sea, there was far land.
There were lost leaves and sinking sand.
Coconut would be a tasty treat.
Tip it, sip it, and scrape to eat.

How little did he know of the sea.
Maybe sharks or mermaids he would see.
No thorns or vines about his feet.
Only little things to ponder and eat.

Another arm would be nice to use.
That would, oh yes, be the greatest news.
But now do his very eyes deceive him?
A tree leaned on his final swim?

WINTER LIFE MUST ENDURE

All day I roam in my cozy home,
Across the chalked wall I do still roam.
House so large that I am the mouse,
Trapped right inside my brittle house.

Flutter page to page to take me home,
From negated stone to a hopeful dome.
Dispirited ears I hold close to mind,
Eyes stay stationed. Failure to the blind.

Windy winter moan howls a scary tale,
Sunlight beats my lizard skin house to ail.
Sun-like petals of open dandelions,
Gather in the lawn like prides of lions.

I know every pinhole and carpet stitch,
Where to find sun rays when the seasons switch.
I know every cringe spot and dusty place,
And the filth I feel when maggots race.

You see… stones strike me as I fret.
I feel left out. Who am I? A pet?
Squash this roach. Where is my room? Sad. So sad.
Frames tilted with splintered glass over years of
glad.

The page turns. I fall asleep in my home.
I will awaken outside and roam, roam, roam.

THE SYMPTOMS OF EARTH

Plants know what the world feels when their roots grow.
Blunt dark with a mighty pulse, earth knows all.
Roots doctor reports of what we don't know.

Worm met root to describe a fair-skinned foe.
Animal with long things shrunk grass, once tall.
Plants know what the world feels when their roots grow.

Soil-sprinkled gophers made talk on tip toe.
Air hole for earth ogre pushed closed with spall.
Roots doctor reports of what we don't know.

Earth's water wept a story mugged of flow.
Better days before earth came to a crawl.
Plants know what the world feels when their roots grow.

Earth's friends engraved legends so roots all know.
What's done before they are bones sheathed in a stall.
Roots doctor reports of what we don't know.

Atop a dying oak sits a very old crow.
Beware of earth's subtle green-less last call.
Plants know what the world feels when their roots grow.
Roots doctor reports of what we don't know.

FIRE IS USEFUL

Bones thrown to flames, now is ash and dust
Amongst the land it makes fruit trees robust
Awake to look for something sweet
Whoever knew we were so good to eat

DRAGON'S NIGHT GLOW

A fly stopped on a dragon toe
We need the nighttime sky to glow
I sailed the knights across the bay
The land is yours to take away

THE FLOATING ISLAND

An island floats about the sea
With gems beneath its mango tree
Without a map to find the land
Look out across the shore and stand

COFFEE HAS MY EYES

When Cocoa made a coffee pie
She got some cream and had a try
And when she got to work she said
Farewell to sleep at home in bed

THE PEPPER SEA

Pepper spiced a sea of pickles
Filled of fish with shiny nickels
Penguins showed the fish the shore
To buy some salt to sneeze no more

120

LIVE WITHIN YOUR BUBBLE SHELL

Pop two bubbles filled with fairies
Flush the soup of rainbow berries
Grab a net and twist in circles
Stop in time, live life like turtles

THE MIDGET FEATHER

Puzzle found a midget feather
Affixed it to his wing, bad weather
Before he flew above the wall
He backed about and had a fall

APPLE ATE A CHERRY

Captain Apple had a cherry
Took a bite, it made him merry
A lumpy woman came by to cook
And grabbed him fast to have a look

THE YUMMY STEW

Forty eyeballs trailed the spoon
And watched the boiling stew lagoon
Noodles filled the bubbling bath
To witness life is simple math

THE DAY OF THE BLUE JAY

Blue Jay found a bumblebee nest
Tweeted loud and fluttered on west
Drinking aside the laughing trout
Singing songs to crickets about

THE LIZARD WHO LOOKED

A lizard looked behind a rock
To find an armless dancing clock
And there upon a wart-less toad
He showed us all a timeless road

PEBBLES CAN BE DEADLY

Scoop up all the violent pebbles
Launch them, yes, straight at the rebels
Victory sealed does come with caution
As someone drops into a coffin

FOR THE KIN

Complicated pill bought for the kin
The nickname given to Jeff's good men
Was formed from the spot that no one thought
It had him fooled, thought tense with fraught

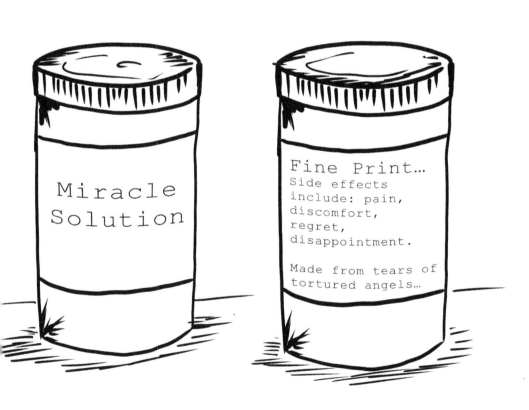

WHEN DO I BLINK?

To blink into a wishing field
Vanishing mushrooms bow and yield
Follow railroads to Sapphire Valley
But do blink twice before tear alley

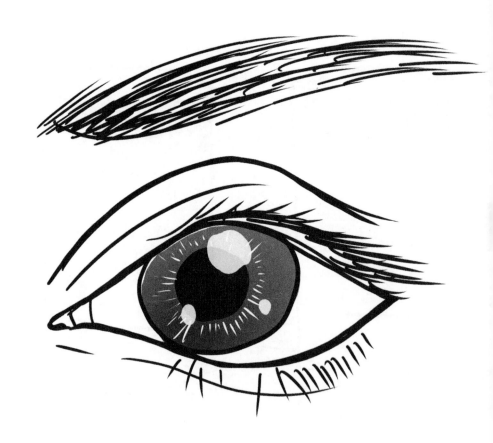

MISS SEA BREEZE

Ms. Sea Breeze, can I get a whiff?
The shore has led me to a cliff
Should I dive in with open eyes
Or will the pain be too unwise?

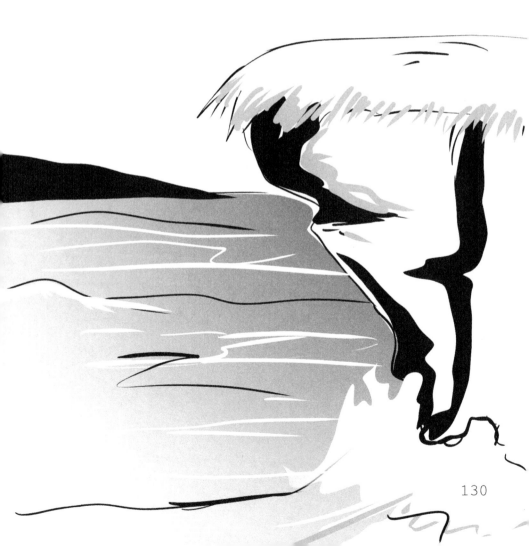

WHAT IS IN YOUR CLOUD?

```
I can walk down a creek and sink
Or climb a cloud compressing ink
When rain does fall, it paints like art
Or makes us blind and makes us part
```

131

TOO MANY RIDDLES IN LIFE

Riddles written on pearls from seas
I found them buried in roots of peas
Nails fractured and dented dug earth away
Deeper and deeper, I dug every day

I WANT MY MIND BACK

They told me I could be what I wanted.
Perhaps an ocean covered with bees.
Still, I do feel I grew as they wanted.
In the shadowed night, my life on its knees.

I went to class so they might feel whole.
I scribbled, I printed; Maybe the wrong way.
Deep down inside, there was a deep hole.
As I now observe searching for a new day.

The roots, the worms, forever no light.
Day will come soon when darkness has fallen.
Strong with light and ready to fight.
To see leaves' and flowers' life in pollen.

Night will be great, they all had told me.
Night, tar, and feathers are what I saw coming.
Sandals and shorts for the night there before me.
The bloom of the flower. The night will go running.

JOURNEY MADE BRIGHT

A frog and a turtle walked all night.
Two ways around stood there before them.
Journey made bright by the fireflies' light.

"We'll walk around," said the green-shelled turtle.
"Getting around this pond will be no hurdle."
A frog and a turtle walked all night.

"I can swim," said the wart-covered frog.
"But there might be snakes in that floating log."
Journey made bright by the fireflies' light.

Branches hung low with spiders lurking.
Turtle shell protection kept on working.
A frog and a turtle walked all night.

A firefly said, "Keep going, keep coming."
With one big hop, a swan came running.
Journey made bright by the fireflies' light.

They made it around the snake-filled pond.
They were off and away with no magic wand.
A frog and a turtle walked all night.
Journey made bright by the fireflies' light.

IT IS YOU

I cut my hair short to make it to you
And add with your divine approval.
I made lions purr and giraffes bow for you,
The jewel-covered maid with an eye for I.
For the wicked, a heart from the man in the can,
Covered in the hog skin once worn by me.
Bees glitter me with a honey tan,
But no more beautiful than open sea.
I wrestled whales and crushed the rolling waves,
With the beauty of your restless heart is where I start.
I stood at the slapping shore, gripping doors to caves.
My crown. It cracks the sandy wind apart.
With the loud silence of my new heart.
Ask, ask. You I must ask.
"Please my queen, destroy your mask."

THE VALLEY NIGHT

Wind-battered waves of flame.
They danced along flesh.
The blue moon pushed sky clouds away.
Bats darted between shimmering blue stars.
Rats seesawed up a valley granite cliff.
Boney claws clinched over leafless branches.
Vampires dangled in suspense to resume debating.
Branches tilted underneath the leafless canopy.
A maple tree rooted on the creek bed.
Bats debating.
Life debating.
Rats retaking the bloodless dead.

THE "S" SOUNDS

```
                    skillfully
            skip              smooth
          stones                    softly
        so                          splashing
      smiles
       shine
        skyward,
          so
            swimming
              souls
                sleep
                  silently
                    setting
                    stationary
      standing      souls
    sipping          sizzling
     salted                soup,
      still                   so
        such              simple
         sing             song
           sounds        soak
                 soon
```

THE MOST BEAUTIFUL MOTHER

My mother had me.
Her belly a dark plum.
Her teeth crafted bars of ivory soap.
I'm warmed by her motherly waves.
Beneath her shaded wing
I slept a peaceful night.
Her hair a coffee black
Sits upon her rolling shoulders
And shines like motor oil
With a feather touch.

She stands as a yellow tulip.
Her contrast bolts across the greenest park.
Her voice a kitten purr,
Hoots in the dark of the night.

Nutritious tears drop
For my trivial accomplishments
That fed my belief,
That grew in the fertile societies of the world.

The sun is jealous of her rays,
And the stars whisper in envy at her guiding light,
And the universe fumbles beyond words to explain
Her love,
A mother's love.

And me
On one knee,
Grateful
For all she had taught me.

YOU WENT WITH THE WIND I THINK

It has been no more than a movie for me.
I watched you,
And I laughed with you.
Your hair was as long as my cat's tail,
As thick as spaghetti noodles.
A foe in game you were.
An ally in war you stood,
And now the fallen leaves wait for you at my door,
Whispering in the wind.

The tree branches yearn for your climbing hand.
Pigeons rest on bending trees,
Waiting for us.

You went away one evening,
As we were closest.
You vanished
Like a raindrop that falls into the sea.
I couldn't find you…

139

WHEN WILL I SEE YOU LOVE?

I can only recall how I held the back of your neck that
day
Underneath the weeping willow tree.
Your skin as soft as a squirrel's tail.
Your lips
As full as a Georgia peach.
Your voice as sweet as pumpkin pie.

But now my throat cramps
As I search.
It's so hard without you, my love.
My
Violet pearl.
My
Shooting star.
My eyes now reside in a rain forest of tears.
My love

And my feet drag.

When will I see you again?
When will I see you again?
My love

YOUR EYES ARE MY STAR

Let's go out into the blackest night,
Where the whitest rose mirrors the moonlight.
Plum sweet eyes get me home tonight,
And make my valley star light bright.

THE CREEK WHERE I END

I found my finish.
It was where I fish.
My eyes, my eyes, they made a wish.
A silken lily on the bend.
Sorrows in my heart, amend.
A spawn of roots with sunlight power.
Colors over far, this flower.
The mind could. This mind could
Begin to comprehend
The slosh of the creek.
I grabbed it before.
I have before.
I had to be four.
My hands could not recover.
The blind apathy.
Life lost inside,
Inside of me.

FOOD TROUBLE

A silver coin sat in my pocket
I walked through the dented walls
Smells of chicken broth and garlic
Stomach aches led to stalls

MY SMELLY ROCKS

In Little's tiny penny box
Were small smelly rocks.
And on this day, they rolled away
Down the stairs and to the bay.

144

MATERIAL VERSUS HOME

Red rose and shattered rubies play about my veins.
Walking obtuse on cloudy curves, birthing hero veins.
Howling with dazed wolves, I am a lost prince with no cribs.
My copper arteries stuck beneath my obsidian ribs.

A ROLLING MARBLE

I have seen a rolling marble.
It glimmered on its stroll.
Across the black flower garden.
Atop the bridge of the koi pen.

YOU HAVE SEEN YOUR LAST SUNRISE

The leaning tree grows on the golden hill.
The grass, it dies, makes you star-like still.
Rolling hills cradle shadows pierced by your tree line tips.
To know you'll die a tearless death in the valley eclipse.